Yahia Lababidi's latest aphorisms plumb the depths of the soul for hard-won truths to set against glib polemics and easy answers. In these troubled times, they point a path through despair to a better way of being together.

—Ben Grant, author of *The Aphorism and Other Short Forms*

As the world haltingly emerges from the pandemic, the prolific Yahia Lababidi offers us his latest hard-earned insights from a lifetime of contemplating about yearning as a form of devotion, the mystic's orbit between world and God, and the necessity of art as a form of self-care. All these revelations are intensified and purified though the crucible of solitary thought that, as everyone knows, social distancing has forced upon us. In this latest collection, it is manifestly clear that Lababidi communes with his ancestors — a global congregation of poets, philosophers, and aphorists.

—Andrew Hui, author of *A Theory of the Aphorism from Confucius to Twitter*

Yahia Lababidi's nacreous aphorisms give thinking a good name. Truth is beautiful thinking and beautiful thinking is truth in these lyrical, political and personal pensées. The economy of surprise is the stuff of inescapable poetic thought.

—David Lazar, author of *I'll Be Your Mirror*

Like every divine utterance, the only way to honor Lababidi's work is to memorize it. I'm starting today. I am moved, touched and remade by his words, sincerity and truth beyond measure. This has not been an easy time for the world, these words heal.

— Robert Inchausti, author of *The Way of Thomas Merton*

If you love Rumi, adore Khalil Gibran, and revere Hafez, you've now found their contemporary. Lababidi's beautiful spiritual aphorisms delve deep, feed the heart, and seriously nourish the soul.

—Cormac Stagg, author of *The Quest for a Humble Heart*

Previous Endorsements

I find myself pausing everywhere among these wisdoms, wondering why the world stumbles and staggers through such a dark and greedy time when there are people alive with such keen, caring insight… If Yahia Samir Lababidi were in charge of a country, I would want to live there.

—Naomi Shihab Nye, poet, anthologist, and author of *There is No Long Distance Now*

Do you know what an aphorism is?
It's not exactly a Haiku, a proverb, an
axiom, nor a poem, yet it harnesses the
power of all these. Aphorisms are an
ancient form, but its current-day master
is Yahia Lababidi.

—Richard Blanco, Barack
Obama's inaugural poet

Lababidi's meditative formulations
echo the inquiries of the early Greeks,
Confucius, de La Rochefoucauld,
Nietzsche, Pascal and Lao Tzu.

—Ken Rodgers, Kyoto Journal
(Japan)

Lababidi is an aphorist of the
spirit. While his aphorisms have

his personal stamp on them, they also transcend him to speak of timeless truths within the timely. They create microcosms that teach us how to inhabit them. His aphorisms could form a new gnostic religion, and I could dwell a long while inside them. Yahia Lababidi may be our greatest living aphorist.

—Sharon Dolin, poet, translator and aphorist

A collection of Yahia Lababidi's aphorisms is like an atlas of tiny maps, each one guiding us calmly through a network of possibilities to a bright and often unexpected vista. Gem-like... we are confronted with his thinking on silence, pain, forgiveness… love.

— Dr Mathew Staunton, historian, publisher and teacher

Wisdom for Lababidi is on the move, a matter of suppleness rather than rigor, of insights and angles rather than rules. …As intense as his conversation with himself is, it is also kind, tolerant of his own limits and of ours…I give you that expert self-listener, that excellent writer, Yahia Lababidi.

—James Richardson, poet, aphorist, and author of *By the Numbers*

Yahia Lababidi's aphorisms are elegant, thoughtful and wise, written proof that the art of the aphorism is still very much alive.

—James Geary, author of *Wit's End*

Lababidi moves from the aphoristic and the epigrammatic to the suggestive, the lightly hinted, the nuanced, with impressive ease. This is a rare gift, more associated with European writers than with American. This striation of tone, of register, of mood, gives a sense of surprise to his sentences; they spring back to the touch. Sometimes they even seem surprised at themselves… The book becomes an exploration on which the reader embarks. This is one of the elements in collections …I most appreciate—this secret invitation au voyage that the author holds out—and Lababidi does this extremely well, with courtesy as well as cunning.

—Eric Ormsby, poet, scholar, and author of *Ghazali: The Revival of Islam*

A Sufi poet not a poet of Sufism as his writing seems to spring from a well of certainty, not feeling. Taste, not observation. It reads like the Sufi poetry of old, but cast in contemporary language.

—Laury Silvers, author of *The Unseen*

Books have doubtless torn Mr. Lababidi asunder. Exposed here are his insides, the divining entrails of a true believer, a man of great faith in the nobility of the human struggle for understanding and transcendence.

In Mr. Lababidi's case … the stage in which he finds his form as an artist is as an aphorist. It is a calling that lends itself perfectly to the endangered art of conversation.

—Joseph Mackin, author of *Pretend All Your Life*

Quarantine Notes

Aphorisms on
Morality & Mortality

Yahia Lababidi

Fomite
Burlington, VT

ISBN-978-1-959984-22-1
Library of Congress Control Number: 2023939108

Fomite
58 Peru Street
Burlington, VT 05401
www.fomitepress.com

07-07 -2023

Grateful acknowledgement is given to the editors of the following journals, where selected aphorisms from this book first appeared: *World Literature Today, Tiferet, Swedenborg Foundation, Philosophical Investigations, Pensive, Escape into Life, Exacting Clam, ArLiJo, Exquisite Pandemic, Harana Poetry & Metapsychosis Journal.*

When the world pushes you to your knees,
you're in the perfect position to pray.

— Rumi

The dervish is a place over which
something is passing, not a wayfarer
following his own will.

— Al-Hujwiri

To be a poet in a destitute time means:
to attend, singing... the poet in the time
of the world's night utters the holy.

— Martin Heidegger

A few words

Quarantine Notes is how I kept sane and spiritually alive during our global pandemic, when our homes became cocoons for radical transformation.

As barriers dissolved between inner and outer worlds, waking and dreaming, self and others, I felt that the midlife crisis I was experiencing (in my late-forties) was mirrored, globally. The world as I knew it was ending, and it was no longer possible to go back, collectively, to our narrow, destructive, oblivious existence: pre-pandemic.

These are the stories that I told myself to save my life, *Shahrazad*-style, as the days turned to weeks to months to years, and one came to feel like they were existing out of time, in a state of limbo, confronted with mortality. The hope is that my soul's dialogue with itself — in the form of aphorisms in this collection — will also resonate with readers since, for the first time in recent history, we were presented with the inescapable reality of our interdependence.

This global pandemic served as an enforced mass meditation for us all and, because it's not quite over, yet, with its lessons hardly digested, it still remains true that "We must love one another or die."

1

Pandemics are also tests of emotional
intelligence.

2

Patriotism, today, is to be ashamed of
one's country.

3

Imagine if presidential candidates
were required to be educated in
moral philosophy.

4

Strange that truths for some are
blasphemies to others.

5

To ask *Why Me?* prevents the
answer from presenting itself.

6

Radical humility is to entertain the
possibility that our worst detractors
might be right about us.

7

We have rituals because we are
forgetful by nature. Books are
another way of remembering what
we know.

8

You are what you do not post, online.

9

You cannot hear another, while you are speaking. It's the same with the Divine voice. *Listen.*

10

Only love can heal the wounds of love.

11

Our insecurities prevent us from recognizing how dearly we are Beloved.

12

To anticipate the worst is to contribute towards its realization.

13

Our fascination with the monstrous
perpetuates it.

14

Our longings shape our future.
Pessimism poisons life and then
wonders why it chokes.

15

Between decadence and mysticism, a
line as fine as a fissure—the depth of
an abyss...

16

Gains obtained unethically, are
short-lived—even if they last a
lifetime.

17

Always act as if you're being
watched: where the surveillance state
and spiritual state are in agreement.

18

If life has placed you on probation,
best to proceed with added caution.

19

There is no private life; what we do,
in secret, is secreted, publicly.

20

Let he who is without sin complain
about injustice.

21

When we are wrongly accused, the punishment still fits the hidden sin.

22

In the same way that love is regenerative medicine, hate is a degenerative disease.

23

Love has many faces—righteous indignation is one.

24

The master and the novice are not permitted the same mistakes.

25

We have only to falter for sins to
commit themselves.

26

Remember, nobody can help you
but—through Him, alone—anybody
can lend a hand.

27

You cannot ask for Help, then shun
it every time it arrives.

28

Looking a gift horse in the mouth is
the human condition.

29

Tell me, how can you tell the
difference between bed bugs and the
bite of conscience?

30

Integrity is to live in a house built by
words.

31

There is something boring about
evil; it is finite.

32

A note to public scolds and angry
activists: good intentions are often
lost in the spittle.

33

Art for art's sake is a dead end; art for heart's sake is the way out.

34

We inhabit a moral universe—amorality is immorality.

35

Learn to recognize those who wish you success, versus those who long for your ruin. Then, you will better understand the ways of G_d and devil.

36

The difference between success and failure, health and sickness, even life and death, is a matter of stamina and sacrifice.

37

To live heedlessly, while still in harm's way, is to court disaster.

38

Like other forces of nature, sexual impulses are both creative and destructive.

39

The precious few times I've peered into my crystal ball, I could make out the letters T.R.U.S.T.

40

The starved think, differently, than the sated.

41

Inspiration speaks in fits and starts—revealing to us only what is necessary at the time.

42

Nietzsche revised: We have art lest we perish of *untruth*.

43

Jokes are distorting mirrors that reflect our absurdity.

44

If we are willing to sacrifice what is dearest to us, in perfect submission, we discover that we are not required to.

45

No respite in the garden without,
first, struggle in the wilderness.

46

The first step towards Love, the
middle and the last, are non-verbal.

47

Fallen angels bleed.

48

Vices are dangerous because they
lead us to even greater moral injury:
heedlessness and hardness of heart.

Regarding laws: yes, civil disobedience, when necessary, but always spiritual obedience. In the realm of the spirit, only radical acceptance.

50

Strange, the power of the past — how our spiritual ancestors become our future masters.

51

To the humble spirit, criticism is cause for self-contemplation.

52

Wisdom is recovered innocence.

53

Conversation: an encounter between
all that we know and what we are
about to discover.

54

The page is a stage.

55

We live, love and create as best as we
can but, sometimes, in haste — lest
we succumb to the siren call of self-
destruction.

56

For better or worse, we might fall
in love with our prisons, until they
blur our vision and we cannot see the
bars, imagining we are free.

57

As a survival mechanism, self-deception is unsustainable.

58

Said the poet: If I draw upon it wisely, my great capital of pain shall serve me a lifetime…
The mystic nodded.

59

Unattended temples are reclaimed by wilderness.

60

To learn patience, learn to sew… your lips shut.

61

With Inspiration one cannot speak
of leading — only seek to be a
worthy dance partner, capable of
keeping up and being spun like a top.

62

Remarkable the human heart how,
faced with threat of extinction,
defiantly, it blossoms.

63

Counting on large miracles prevents
us from recognizing the countless
small ones, daily, granted.

64

Much of the suffering in our world is the
result of wounded children, parenting.

65

Gratitude: to be thankful for the good, the bad, and what we do not (yet) understand.

66

A working definition of Love: *we started talking and never stopped...*

67

Never mind poetry or prose, good literature is the art of friction.

68

In unlearning, we better appreciate the world on its own terms.

As a profession, constructing sentences is as honorable as building homes — if we and others can live in them.

What is *not* a writing prompt?

Questions as quests.

When you've done all you can, there is nothing left to worry about.

73

The easy way is always harder in the end.

74

Nothing dates so fast as what is up-to-date.

75

Writing is a kind of echolocating —
to discover our tribe.

76

You know someone by the angels and demons that gather around their name.

77

The primary challenge for our survival is resisting self-destruction.

78

One gauge of a person's intelligence (and interestingness) is their comfort level living with Mystery.

79

Spiritual immaturity asks: *Are we there, yet?*

80

One cannot question the miraculous.

81

What an indictment against *reality*, that we spend half our waking hours practicing the vital art of daydreaming.

82

To build up your capacity to say No, begin in your dreams.

83

Forgiveness, human or Divine, might always be granted — but it is never a given.

84

Exiles, always, feel a little posthumous; at heart, we are all exiles…

85

Adolescence: when the wild begins
to call us.

86

Virtuous spirals versus vicious cycles.

87

 As a connoisseur of the abyss, Samuel
Beckett offers us a strange solace. First,
he confirms our worst suspicions about
Life — the absurdity and *nothingness that
show through everything* — then he offers
the bitter relief of cackling it all off, saying:
'Nothing is funnier than unhappiness.'
Becket is all of us, in extremis.

88

To transcend Time, transcend Self.

89

If you do not possess gnostic
certainty, at least resist cynic doubt.

90

Aphorisms are the sushi of literature.

91

Should we forget our body for long,
it will pinch us as a reminder.

92

Poetry-making is a taste of eternity,
and the perpetual freshness of
ancient wisdom.

93

Do not complain to others of your
symptoms, while concealing your
disease.

94

Seek to be, in your self, a community.

95

The inescapable vulnerability of all
who live beneath that tent of blue…

96

Bookshelves are cemeteries, where we
go to visit our past loves.

97

Your attachment to your inner
demons is at the demons' bidding.

98

Tact is getting others to listen.

99

Too much ego, the life suffers. Not
enough, and the art does.

100

Art that is vital remains so across
centuries and millennia.

101

Poetry is what happens to prose at boiling point.

102

Desert: the spiritual sensuality of the world, denuded.

103

In the larger body of a writer's work, include their conversations.

104

In an age of information, knowledge is curation. In the face of excess, balance is abstinence.

105

Silence is sometimes the charitable answer.

106

Unlettered: without recourse to a Divine book.

107

Sacred signs everywhere, yourself among them.

108

The master of darkness is a student of the Light.

109

Recognize the warped virtues within your vices.

110

Silence and Time are wiser than we are.

111

Just as some lust for material wealth, there is also spiritual greed for gnosis.

112

I cannot have what I want: a curse, a blessing.

113

Being frightened by our shadow and making peace with it are not mutually exclusive.

114

Free speech is not an absolute good, nor is censorship an absolute evil.

115

We are moral beings, and words lead to actions.

116

The best type of censorship is self-censorship — aka morality.

117

Spiritually speaking, a sense of independence is a form of arrogance.

118

How we address our pain can help us prolong or overcome it.

119

True solitude is not lonely, it is companionable.

120

To see better, as darkness falls, move closer to the Light.

121

Hope is a virtuoso of patience.

122

The mystery of destiny is that there are no accidents and we are responsible for our lives.

123

Spiritually understood, everything can be used for our development and advantage.

124

The ancients are timeless; it's the ultra-moderns that age fast. *Mortui vivos docent.*

125

Ironic, that we prefer a familiar pain
to unfamiliar joy.

126

We have world wars because empires
require upkeep.

127

Give thanks to all who kept you
from self-destruction — especially
your Creator.

128

Writing is only partially realized
until it's read, and fully so when
lived by.

129

There are prophets not mentioned in
the holy books—who bear witness,
universally, and deliver Divine
messages entrusted to them.

130

There is something of the visionary
in the activist and the martyr, both
willing to devote or sacrifice their
lives for an Ideal.

131

Human ideal: poet's heart,
philosopher's mind, and mystic soul.

132

In the absence of transparency,
conspiracy theories.

133

Even the ritual of turning on your
computer every morning, mindfully,
can be a form of prayer.

134

The punishment for avoiding
suffering is superficiality; the reward
for embracing it is spirituality.

135

Revolution is a kind of drunkenness,
like love. It's difficult to revisit our
sentiments, sober, when it's over.

136

Vastness: our only way out of this
narrow-hearted mess...

Strange, shifting heart... breathlessly
panting after the world in the early
morning and, sublimely rid of it by
afternoon.

138

The ancient Greek root meaning
of "sin" is "missing the mark." For
this reason, judged by a narrow morality,
mystics are sometimes deemed heretics.

139

Chapbook: a full-length book that
grew impatient.

140

We are responsible for our moral
deformity.

141

Brooding—when birds are ready to sit on their eggs and incubate them, while sacrificing most other activities, including feeding and drinking—is an apt metaphor for the commitment, patience and care required of creatives, before hatching a new idea.

142

Lose your self, find your Way.

143

Sometimes, desperation can look like courage.

144

Transgression is a choice, an assent to evil suggestion.

145

Too much questioning is a sign of spiritual immaturity.

146
We work on ourselves so that we might better serve others, and vice versa.

147

The best and most dangerous lies are mixed with truth. It's truth that attracts others and allows them to accept untruths.

148

Cartoon characters run on thin air and fall only once they look down. With us, that fatal downward glance might be the act of doubting The Safety Net.

149

We must do what we can, first,
before we might be helped to do
what we cannot.

150

Critiquing one's nation, the way we
might our family or friends, is still
a form of love and means that we've
not given up on them.

151

Resist cultural encouragement when
it contradicts the innate wisdom of
your temperament.

152

The path less trodden is harder on
the feet, but better for the soul.

153

The interpretation of signs is an
ever-subtle art.

154

Misfortune might be Divine
pleasure, and fortune Divine
dissatisfaction.

155

An affinity exists between
extremes—they are closer to one
another than to moderation.

156

If we understood the great bargain
offered us, we would not waste
another instant in selling the paltry
seen for the riches of the Unseen.

157

Radicalization is a tragic inability to live with uncertainty—the opposite of Aristotle's educated mind, able to entertain a thought without accepting it.

158

Even sages are novices, in relation to the Absolute…

159

The same way that the heart wants what it wants, the mind also needs what it needs.

160

Everything contains the secret to everything else.

To Believe is to know, is to
understand.

Poetry is the mother tongue of
prophesy.

Where there are demons, there is
something precious worth fighting
for. Why else would so many spirits
battle over one soul?

Poets are the unacknowledged
Ministers of Loneliness.

165

There are no secrets. Soft whispering behind the backs of others, even dark thoughts, are secreted through shifty eyes, the guile of a smile, and suspect actions.

166

Try and think well of others. Suspicion betrays a mistrust of oneself.

167

Walk so that you don't frighten small birds away.

168

Art is the finest form of cultural diplomacy.

169

Historical amnesia: how people get retraumatized.

170

The arguments of atheists grow old, the older they get.

171

Eloquence of disbelievers pales in comparison to even the mumbling of mystics.

172

Love is not a part-time job.

173

'Ink, if not used, will dry up' says a
Polish proverb. I take this to mean
the life that we do not live and the
love we do not give...

174

Two ways through — one fiendishly
difficult, the other utterly simple: the
ways of the head and heart.

175

If you feel you've wasted much time
getting started, don't waste more.

176

Birds don't use their wings only to fly
but, also, for balance—just like us.

177

Might cancel culture be another term for Karma?

178

The Truth, like Moses' staff which transformed into a mighty serpent, will devour all sorcerers' deceptions.

179

Only the weak in faith mistake mere magic for a miracle.

180

Take your dreams seriously, they represent unfinished work. But don't take them too seriously — they represent unfinished work.

181

Riddles don't yield to rough,
impatient fingers.

182

What can artists do in times of
crises? Offer art as blood transfusion
and even heart transplant!

183

Disappointment is a function of
expectation.

184

Strange, how what is life-giving — if
not handled with care — can become
life-threatening.

185

Self-pity: the flip side of egoism.

186

Shameless: the new normal.

187

Wisdom is remembering all we know.

188

There is a hopeful waiting, akin to prayer, that wards off despair.

189

Aphorisms are a blurring of borders: wisdom literature meets psychological observation, or philosophy cloaked as poetry that is spiritually-informed.

190

Sometimes, the crack in everything lets the light in — other times, it's darkness.

191

With despair as with night-vision, the eyes soon grow accustomed to the dark.

192

Perhaps we attract certain poems to us the way we do love or friendship or luck.

193

Whisper, He is near, and can hear.

194

How we squander eternal currency
in life's bustling marketplace…

195

Gratitude entails action, charity.

196

Writing advice: the bride is the
page—revere it, make love to it.

Perhaps the widespread use of
the word "awesome" is a kind of
unconscious secular prayer.

198

If language is the house of being,
glibness is a construction hazard.

199

For words to remain sacred, we must
exercise restraint and sometimes
practice silence.

200

A fling is not a relationship, even if it
lasts years.

201

We reinvent ourselves in order to
survive, when we arrive at a dead end.

202

However we scheme or dream, being
reborn is always a surprise.

203

Do not lose hope or become
arrogant—the wind may turn.

204

It's not what we've done, but what
remains undone, that weighs on us.

205

What human treatment for heavenly affliction?

206

Disappearing is difficult, daily work. But the alternative is harder to live with.

207

For exiles, the cost of a new life is an enduring sense of betrayal or survivor's guilt.

208

Exiles speak a special language that only exiles understand.

209

New Age: old wine, much diluted.

210

We unburden ourselves when we lighten the load for others.

211

Seeming contradictions and paradox are at the heart of life's mysteries. Such teaching by means of opposites drew me first to Nietzsche, then to the Tao te Ching, and finally home to Sufism.

212

Please, Covid, in the words of Blaise Pascal: *Teach us the proper use of sickness.*

213

There's freedom in limitations, even liberation in deprivations.

214

Fold vast wings into your words, so that those who hear them might be elevated.

215

Inertia increases our labor; as deadlines loom, we are unfit to complete the work.

216

A death might be an occasion to discover a life.

217

So many vows, written in
disappearing ink…

218

Hell is being trapped in the vicious
cycle of our vices.

219

Life lesson from raising pigeons:
They don't just fly away one day.
Taking to the air takes much practice
and, afterwards, constant grooming
of feathers.

220

The danger of cynicism is getting
what you believe in: Nothing.

221

Imagination: imagine a nation.

222

Self-care is not a luxury, but a
necessity—to better care for others.

223

Making people laugh or helping
them smile are acts of charity, like
clothing and feeding the poor.

224

Our helplessness allows Grace to
take place.

225

What do humans want? To be
shown how to endure suffering with
courage, grace and a smile.

226

It is not true repentance when one
has no other alternatives.

227

Deep devotion produces great art.

228

Heaven save us from the literalists,
who have reduced the rich
symbolism and poetry of faith to
murderous condemnation.

229

Abstinence, for some, is the
aphrodisiac of the soul.

230

Poems seem to grow with us. Often,
it is only we who are catching up
with a poem's dimension.

231

Miracles are easier on all fours.

232

Stillness is silence made visible.

233

Without silliness, no seriousness.

234

Our suffering is alleviated when assigned meaning.

235

Don't put others to the test; they might disappoint.

236

Content yourself with being a connoisseur of failure and small success.

237

To speak of spiritual intimations is a kind of kiss and tell.

238

Great art is a type of mummification of the Spirit.

239

Real love is beyond desire and self-interest.

240

Spiritual love regards the Beloved above all.

241

In human relations, awe prevents recognition; while in Divine affairs, it grants true perception.

242

Words seem to reinvent us just as we think we are inventing them.

243

Just as with alcohol, there are those who get drunk too easily, too quickly... on words.

244

At times, bodies speak their own language and seem to have their own minds.

245

In a popular culture that rewards
instant gratification and indulgence,
it becomes harder to find heroes that
represent restraint, abstinence or
sacrifice.

246

Should your life appear mean or
narrow, pay closer attention to the
richness of your unlived life.

247

We are haunted by the ghosts of who
we meant to be.

248

Cover the faults of others, as yours
have been covered by the Divine.

249

As you might imagine, much of the poetry does not make it onto the poem...

250

Faithlessness is forgetfulness; we already agreed to bow—before Time began.

251

The worst type of monster is a helpless one. (And all monsters are helpless.)

252

There are sins in humans—such as, jealousy and pride—that are virtues of the Divine.

253

The anxiety of atheists stems from rebellion against their own natural state: submission to the Divine.

254

Love is shy, until it deepens. It's the same with love for the Divine.

255

It is not the transient body that smiles at death, but the eternal soul.

256

By making ourselves available to life's extremes—not shielding ourselves from dangerous experiences—we are granted illuminations.

257

There's no deadline for appreciation.

258

You cannot rush inspiration; the Noble Quran was revealed over twenty-three years.

259

When we sin, we invite it to return, again.

260

It's necessary to practice a holy monotony as part of an uninterrupted sacred conversation.

261

All of life is unrelenting spiritual warfare.

262

The older I get, and the more I observe popular culture, the better I appreciate Plato's criticism of art and its ability to destroy the moral fabric of society.

263

Art is a powerful illusion and thus potentially dangerous. We are, after all, what we consume.

264

My life is an open book: Facebook.

265

Reading the Quran, in quarantine,
and breathing easier.

266

In the realm of the esoteric, the
master is merely a disciple.

267

To dedicate one's life solely to art is
to be a choosey beggar.

268

A free person takes no psychological
prisoners.

269

Making poetry is another way of making love.

270

We should ration our silences, the way we do words.

271

When we vacate ourselves and listen is when we are most likely to receive insights.

272

If you wish to court the Divine, imagine how much truer you must be than if you were to woo another human.

273

Even Divine silence is providential.

274

Strange, that for certain Vision
to occur, there should be a partial
blindness.

275

We might not care for
psychoanalysis; but we cannot afford
to not attend to our dreams.

276

A conscious person living among
the unconscious is like a sober driver
navigating drunkards.

277

In art, as in life, there is freedom within restrictions.

278

Blasphemy: to assume that what we do not understand is meaningless.

279

Mirrors, like photographs, are a trap—in how they fix us in place.

280

A believer is like a person in love: invincible in a sense, and helpless before the Beloved.

281

If wisdom governs us, one day, it
might governments.

282

Proceed with caution, then abandon.

283

Arrogance is to ignorance as humility
is to wisdom.

284

Hope is available in great abundance
the closer we are to the Source.
What life-coaches offer is merely
the shadow of hope and light. Yet,
genuine seeking is hard work, so the
masses settle for pastiche spirituality
and diluted philosophy instead.

No matter how barren the landscape
appears, we are always sitting on gold
— which we can reach through hard
work and devotion.

A mystic is a person who has
discovered something more
interesting than sex.

There are many types of ignorance;
the loudest is arrogance.

The word of God is not revealed all
at once, but rationed in mysterious
portions.

289

Some eyes are pools; others are schools.

290

When the wronged don't retaliate, it invites Divine intervention.

291

Style: the garment we shed on our way to nakedness.

292

Sleep, daily, prepares us for dying.

293

O, the brethren of solitaries,
sleepwalkers and day dreamers. If
only they knew how many they
were—they might take courage in
their numbers and, who knows, even
feel a sense of belonging?

294

Hope is waiting without losing faith.

295

Cowards are hard of heart; the
courageous, tender-hearted.

296

To despair, hate, or seek revenge is to
be seduced by evil.

297

Mouths may mislead, but eyes never lie.

298

For God's fools, the hard is made easy.

299

Metaphors, like all possible explosives, should be handled with care, and by those who know what they're doing.

300

Unattended baggage is spiritually dangerous.

301

We neglect to give thanks not because of the scarcity of our blessings, but because of their overwhelming abundance (which we take for granted).

302

The omnipresence of blessings makes them invisible.

303

Daily, we are assisted by benevolent, mysterious forces.

304

Perhaps, on some level, there are only inner conversations, and outer ones are merely extensions of these.

305

Sometimes, our undeveloped ideas
blossom with caring souls; other
times, they wither in unsympathetic
hands.

306

It takes guts, and imagination, to
invent ourselves — our limitations
are our longings.

307

Anything freed from the marble is an
angel. Never cease chiseling...

308

Distance affords clarity and charity.

309

It's better to be good than great.

310

Whatever harm occurs to our
perishable selves is reversible,
only if we are anchored in the
Indestructible.

311

O, this blessed, cursed world…

312

Religion: the science of morality.

313

It should not be difficult to understand addiction. We are all addicted, in varying degrees, to life's illusions.

314

Beauty is a synonym for virtue.

315

If we are susceptible to praise, we are vulnerable to blame.

316

One day, leaf. One day, branch. One day, root.

317

If not humility, then humiliation.

318

Maybe steadfastness, courage, and patience are different names for the same thing.

319

The way we open up after (self) forgiveness…

320

One sign of a healthy, fulfilling personal life is that it is not performed online. (The more that it is, the less it is…)

321

Forgiveness, like Grace, is not
entirely up to us…

322

To think ourselves *the worst* is,
perversely, to privilege ourselves—a
distortion and exaggeration of our
importance.

323

Silence is worth thousands of words.

324

Being hostage to beauty: the strength
and weakness of artists.

325

Falling can seem like flying — for a while.

326

We are granted spiritual gifts in relation to our sacrifices.

327

Respect what your gray hair is telling you.

328

Just as the seen is a fraction of the Unseen, so the revealed is only a portion of the Unrevealed.

329

Revelation is a reminder of what we know.

330

We are careful with what we eat and drink so as not to poison our body—yet we do not consider how what we consume through our eyes or ears might corrupt our spirit.

331

We are tasked to become endurance artists.

332

There's something about the desert that collapses the distinction between real and metaphorical.

333

Sometimes it's only when a blessing becomes absent that it becomes apparent.

334

Do not be so invested in this world that you reject the summons of the Next…

335

Mystic: someone who has discovered something more interesting than thinking.

336

If you ask to be raised in spiritual station, expect trials to match such an elevation.

337

By enduring severe trials, patiently,
we recognize that they are blessings.

338

Angelology: a caste system.

339

Court jesters are unacknowledged
kings.

340

How can artists not believe in the
impossible, when their innermost
vulnerabilities might be transformed
into art that inspires strangers.

341

If we look at ourselves deeply, we
pardon others.

342

If we look even deeper, we realize
that there are no others...

343

When we give more than we can afford
— as a gesture of goodwill, trust,
forgiveness, even —it is returned in
kind. Generosity begets generosity.

344

Just as we can become desensitized
to violence, we might also grow
accustomed to decadence — until
amorality appears to us a natural state.

345

One cannot serve two masters: a
sensualist is not a spiritualist.

346

When the world is ending, propose a
toast to *New Beginnings*.

347

We kiss and pray with our eyes shut
for the same reason: the Beloved is
formless.

348

Prayer beads: squeezing divine teats
for heavenly milk.

349

The visible and invisible are indivisible.

350

Mystics, like all lovers, must consent to be annihilated.

351

Gender equality is a reality — in the next world.

352

Stagnation: the enemy of evolution.

353

There are countless prophets,
unknown to us, who work in secret.

354

We are granted different powers to
help one another.

355

Old age and misfortune teach us:
invisible gifts might be gained, when
visible ones are confiscated.

356

Lostness: confounding the counsel
of the devil assigned you with that of
your guardian angel.

357

What makes for much dangerous
confusion in the spheres of religion,
politics, and what passes for love, is a
patina of goodness.

358

To resist diseases of the heart,
cultivate spiritual immunity.

359

Hate is a sickness of the soul.
Tolerance does not debate this in the
marketplace of ideas.

360

Fear of hunger and lust for satiety
are enemies of Longing.

361

In love and war: getting in is easy,
but when and how we get out can be
catastrophic…

362

The first steps towards love, the
middle, as well as the last, are
nonverbal.

363

The best poems need not be
written—they are meant to rewrite
our souls.

364

For those who can read the signs,
cosmos is scripture.

365

The straight path is available to all who forsake crookedness.

366

Do not let trials alter your trust in Him.

367

Distance from Him is also distance from our true selves.

368

We slide into cynicism, but must climb towards Hope.

369

That elusive balance: some days, silence, and stillness; others, communication, and commotion.

370

Imagine a world where the worst insult was: *inelegant*.

371

The desert is wise like someone who had and lost it all — becoming a witness, outliving itself.

372

Because there's no place to hide in the desert, it is where we go to seek ourselves and dissolve…

373

Bless the anonymous pious; their presence among us serves as spiritual protection.

374

The vision shall be fulfilled, but not when or how we expect.

375

Let humiliation be your teacher.

376

The resurgence of spirituality—real and diluted—is a counterbalance to cynicism.

377

Cynicism is a degenerative disease.

378

True poets, like mystics, are
messenger pigeons.

379

When in doubt, be patient and
praise.

380

Learn to recognize the spiritual
benefit in affliction.

381

The danger of minor transgressions
is that they might lead to larger vices.

382

Those with apparent contradictions
are better equipped to understand
life's inherent paradoxes.

383

In life, there are no contradictions,
only paradoxes.

384

Question the whispered suggestion
and ask: *Revelation from whom?*

385

Even prophets are susceptible to the
Deceiver.

386

In the mystery of timing, we glimpse
the invisible hand of God at work.

387

What is *not* conjecture, save true
Inspiration?

388

Half an hour of epiphany is enough
to draw upon for an entire life.

389

Heartbreak is not the end of Love…

390

Books upon books can be composed discussing the relation between Divine determinism and human choice—but silence is more eloquent.

391

Surrender: the paradox of *Free Will*.

392

We are unfree when we stray from Divine Will.

393

What you consider a moment of awakening might, in fact, be one of spiritual devolution.

394

Detachment, paradoxically, might be the ultimate engagement with life—unconditional loving, unconcerned with results.

395

We inhabit ourselves more fully when we can find our inner light switches in the dark...

396

Maturity is a faith-filled life.

397

Silence is a powerful punctuation
mark.

398

What our body cannot use, it flushes
out. It's the same with our Spirit.

399

Hope is how we renew our vows
with life.

400

Good artists are heralds of the world
to come.

401

Every culture, closely examined, is Janus-faced.

402

Spirituality is not a costume party.

403

Even prophets know only what they are told.

404

Philosophers might be a hairline away from prophecy — were they not too proud to identify as mere messengers...

405

Independence within interdependence.

406

When the student is not ready,
imposters appear.

407

In every discipline, spirituality
included, there are masters and
students; part of the problem with
our confused, cynical times is
disputing this self-evident truth.

408

A prophet waiting for revelation
is a person reminded of their utter
dependence and helplessness.

409

There is a realm of reality where poetry is found; poets merely dip their pens in invisible ink.

410

Trusted, Time is a partner in our maturity.

411

Nations fail for the same reason that people fall: they lose their balance.

412

Trying is not losing.

413

Where there is Love, there is
relenting.

414

When we repent, He relents.

415

We are taunted by the distance
between our best insights and our
foolishness.

416

Wisdom of aging: a darkening brain
in exchange for an illumined heart.

417

Our willingness to readily believe the worst of others speaks badly of us.

418

If you cannot do good, at least, practice biting your tongue.

419

Pursuit of an Ideal, without discernment, becomes grotesque.

420

Men may fight battles, but it's angels that win wars.

421

The prophet and the poet are the shell: Divine song is the kernel.

422

Worldliness: short-sightedness.

423

So many virtual relations, offline.

424

So many real relations, online…

425

Lazy autodidact is an oxymoron.

426

Mystics: they who surrender their
passion to the Lord.

427

The spiritual journey is one of risk—
in perpetual danger of spilling over
the edge…

428

In our dreams, we are not free from
battling demons or hosting angels.

429

When we are mortally wounded
by those dearest to us, the knives of
strangers draw no blood.

430

In imperiled states, the soul defends
itself with poetry.

431

Pain is the signal of a soul in distress;
spiritual numbness signifies its death.

432

Doubt, as a season of the soul, is
like a strong wind that prunes trees
— loosening dead leaves and weak
branches — to fortify our foundation
against future storms of the spirit.

433

Why complain to others when
they cannot help you? Address the
Knower of all hearts' secrets.

434

Hunger, as a metaphor, for artists
and all seekers.

435

It is a sign of decadence when
there is more moral outrage over
sex confusion than over poverty, or
blasphemy, or murder.

436

Since they are primarily interested
in themselves, narcissists make poor
judges of character.

437

Forgetfulness is a type of ingratitude,
Remembrance a form of prayer.

438

It probably wasn't as bad (or good)
as we remember. Memory can be
trusted… to embellish.

439

We live and unlearn.

440

When we begin by abusing ourselves,
we end up abusing others.

441

Strangely, androgyny and
renunciation go hand in hand.

442

Of all books, my favorites echo
Silence.

443

You make your bed every day—why
not pray?

444

It's a sign of guilt to readily pardon
the sins of others.

445

As our mind and spirit change shape,
our style follows.

446

Monsters sympathize with other
monsters.

447

Between the arbitrary judgements
of audience and artists, there
remains two arbiters of taste and
endurance: the discerning critic and
incorruptible Time.

448

It's the harpoon that makes the Prey
elusive.

449

Even insects are attracted to the
Light and, entrapped in darkness,
will beat their heads or wings —
frantic to escape.

450

Remembering how far we've come, a
spur to how far we can go.

451

Hope is waiting… without losing
hope.

452

Gradual revelation strengthens the
heart.

453

Mental hygiene is inseparable from
spiritual hygiene.

454

The trick is not to think of others
when we write, so as not to give
ourselves stage-fright or falsify feelings.

455

If only we were less impatient,
greedy, doubtful... we might be
granted a greater Joy than our stolen
paltry pleasures.

456

Perhaps, on some level, there's only
the inner conversation, the outer
ones mere echoes.

457

Poetry is eternal currency.

458

Think of your pain as a physician, diagnosing your sickness, and guiding you to health.

459

Poets might be prophets, but their houses are in disarray and lives rarely equal to their insights.

460

All arts are secondary to the art of living.

461

Forgive the polluted streams, says
the sea, they must endure their own
poison.

462

To the religious, "spiritual" sounds
like "agnostic."

463

Necessity is the mother of invention
also applies to the art of self-
invention.

464

How do you survive another broken-
heart after, finally, daring to Hope,
again? A question for lovers and
revolutionaries.

465

Read the one book that rids you of spiritual clutter.

466

Each day whispers, to those who listen: This, is what is being asked of you, now.

467

A day is considered wasted if one does not make contact with the Indestructible Beauty, in this world and the next.

468

The connoisseur of dead ends points the Way Out.

469

We have art as consolation for not flying.

470

In a sense, no metamorphosis is ever complete...

471

Prayer as a first and last resort—in between, action.

472

Stagnation is a lie. What does not evolve, will atrophy.

473

Luck: another name for Grace.

474

Chance: another word for Destiny.

475

Remind the wounded child of their
ever-merciful parent: G_d.

476

We are as profound as our silences.

477

Humility, in the realm of the Spirit,
is always to imagine that the other
person might know more than you
do.

478

Distrust the false assurances of
pessimism.

479

Cynicism is unwise—a human
failing.

480

Free people free people.

481

The secret inscribed upon our inner tablet takes a lifetime to decipher.

482

Try not to forget the near shipwreck when, safely, on shore. On land, you still might encounter earthquakes.

483

Pleasure is amoral, happiness is moral.

484

The one who sells the world is without remorse. A true renunciant is not reluctant.

485

We are deluded in thinking there are
choices other than surrender.

486

Unfreedom: identifying with a
position of rebellion.

487

Go back into the fire of childhood
and rescue yourself.

488

What is permissible for others might
be impermissible for you.

489

In the worldly, as in the spiritual,
sobriety follows intoxication.

490

The insights of intoxication are
realized in sobriety.

491

The unwritten is the iceberg, writing
merely the tip.

492

Only what is infinite in us can grasp
the Infinite.

493

Silence is a language with many
dialects.

494

Strange world of paradoxes — on
one hand, the path to peace is self-
forgetfulness; on the other, it is self-
remembering.

495

Say visible
(whisper invisible)
confess indivisible.

496

Agnosticism: a failure of
imagination.

497

Part of the secret seduction of evil is
truth, distorted.

498

Curators: our guides in the age of
information overload.

499

Longing, the undertow of Being,
beckoning…

500

Investigate, with tender curiosity,
where flesh and spirit meet.

501

Your shortcomings as a person are your limitations as a writer.

502

What is unbecoming is what prevents us from Becoming.

503

This world is filled with otherworldly beauty.

504

In unlearning what we have learned, we better appreciate the world, on her terms.

505

Behind attraction, even erotic, is a
disguised lust for self-knowledge.

506

Consistent results replicated across
studies are said to have scientific
merit. By association, I think of the
consistently calming, centering effect
of prayer, across traditions.

507

The easy way — enmity,
estrangement — is harder in the
long run.

508

Heart is where the home is.

509

Pity the immigrant their exile from Home. Those who survive, die several small deaths.

510

When we recognize that we hurt ourselves when we hurt others, we begin to live differently.

511

It's a perversity of human nature how, despite the evidence, we persist in thinking the best of ourselves —while vilifying others, for behaving as we do.

512

No lasting freedom can be founded upon the suffering of others.

513

We are expelled from paradise every time we forget. We return to heaven when we Remember.

514

Ethics: Freedom within limitations.

515

Strong medicine, in the wrong hands, is poison.

516

We ought to not ask for better fortune but try and be worthy of the good fortune we already possess.

517

Before we can bend our knee, we
must bend our will.

518

Aphorisms are seeds carrying
orchards.

519

In healing ourselves, we heal others.

520

Poetry is ministry.

Afterword by Andrew Benson Brown

The future is that almost invisible
line of letters at the bottom of
the eye chart: nearly everyone
who squints toward it wears dark
sunglasses or rose-colored spectacles
to overcompensate for a naked
myopia. Most rosy viewers fall into
the category of the shallow optimist,
a sanguine temperament brightened
by social beliefs that see no problem
with things continuing the way they
always have in the past. Whether
that collective perpetuation is one
of automatic progress or reactionary
stagnation, the accompanying
mental experience is self-delusion.

The pessimists, viewing life through shades as black as a moonless midnight, imagine themselves to be clear-eyed realists. Despite this, their spectral realignment is not as blind as the average optimist's. Everywhere they look there seems to be cause for despair. While claims to cross-cultural understanding are legion, tribalism dominates our century. Extremist factions on every side of the political spectrum, so quick to denounce the dangerous tenets of their enemies, are blind to the repressive aspects of their own creeds. Riots, mass shootings, human trafficking, suicide bombings and civil wars all attest to a world riven by hatred. Beyond this, the twin threats of nuclear war and environmental degradation highlight the very real possibility of humanity's extinction.

Yahia Lababidi does not wear dark sunglasses. His shades are not only rosy—they cast rainbows on their horizon. Yet he somehow manages not to be trite or shallow in his appraisals, and even to be the opposite. His wisdom has an ancient quality that speaks to the present about its future. He readily acknowledges that, "The primary challenge for our survival is resisting self-destruction." But at the same time he admonishes, "Pessimism poisons life and then wonders why it chokes." Though the COVID-19 outbreak was a catalyst for violence and political polarization, the aphorisms collected in this book exemplify the positive consequences of quarantine. Famines sometimes bear strange fruit. Solitude can lead to reflection, crises to personal breakthroughs. Lababidi shows us that there is something beyond our mundane, everyday reality, a place untouched by evil, anger, and other spiritually corrupting influences.

His vision is the mystic's vision. His cognitive faculty is intuition, a mode of divine communication which requires a corresponding method of literary delivery to be effective. In order to express direct insight and encourage its adoption in the reader, one cannot be too wordy. Where the

logical proposition is like a saw or a
hatchet, chipping away at its log of
truth bit by bit to build its argument,
the aphorism is like a hammer. It
may not fell a tall tree like a long
analytical treatise, but it will knock
a nail into place and help secure a
small part of a structure's integrity.
Or perhaps the aphorism is the
nail and the mystic is the hammer.
Whichever way one chooses to
emphasize the analogy, it is a tool
with a wider application than that
made famous by Nietzsche in his
mission of demolishing idols.

One must not only smash, but build.
Lababidi shows us the constructive
uses of philosophizing with a
hammer. He emphasizes hope,

self-understanding, tolerance for
uncertainty, light over darkness,
and the moral foundation of being.
Some aphorisms are worded as
truth statements, others as practical
advice. Surface grammar is no
proof of mutual exclusivity: a truth
statement of this type often implies
how one should behave so as to live
in accordance with it. Some of the
sayings have hymn-like qualities,
and a sense of gratitude permeates
the text. We are a long way from the
French salons of the 17th century,
where La Rochefoucauld spouted
his bitter maxims which, for all their
wit and variety, can essentially be
boiled down to the view: "man is a
selfish being." Lababidi's precepts

accumulate towards the opposite conclusion. For him, the self is a thing to be discarded.

Most collections of aphorisms are crowded affairs. As soon as readers finish one they are pushed along to the next, usually with only a single white line to separate them. This book does the opposite. It encourages one to contemplate brevity by quarantining Lababidi's sayings, mirroring the condition of their creation. Lababidi himself puts it in a way that nicely reflects the volume's organization: "Aphorisms are the sushi of literature." A large bite, carefully prepared by a master chef, delicately savored. Wrapped in white space like rice, each piece's placement on the page helps cleanse the palate like a slice of ginger, preparing one for the next bite. Though readers will inevitably douse their sushi in the soy sauce of their peculiar, accidentally-acquired prejudices, the author would encourage light dipping so as to not overwhelm the natural flavor of each insight. There is too much sodium in our diets as it is, too much salt in our worldviews.

The main difference between an aphorism and a proverb is that the latter has entered general use and become part of a culture's vocabulary for expressing its common truths. In Lababidi's case, this is a distinction that is likely to collapse as time passes and his sayings, already widely quoted and translated, become even more generally known. As the global pandemic has shown us, the boundaries between individual and world, one society and another, are more fluid than they are fixed, and different cultures must inevitably come to recognize the truths they share in common if humanity is to survive. Yahia Lababidi can help us achieve this shared self-understanding. His wisdom sits at the intersection of civilizations—past, present, and future.

Andrew Benson Brown
Missouri, 2022

About the Author

Yahia Lababidi, an Egyptian author
of ten collections of poetry and
prose, has been called "our greatest
living aphorist". His aphorisms and
poems have gone viral, are used in
classrooms, religious services, and
feature at international film festivals.

Lababidi has also contributed to news, literary and cultural institutions throughout the USA, Europe and the Middle East, such as: Oxford University, Pearson, PBS NewsHour, NPR, HBO as well as ABC Radio.

His latest work includes *Desert Songs* (Rowayat, 2022), a bilingual, photographic account of mystical encounters in the desert, as well as *Learning to Pray* (Kelsay Books, 2021), a collection of his spiritual reflections.

Fomite

Writing a review on social media sites for readers will help the progress of independent publishing. To submit a review, go to the book page on any of the sites and follow the links for reviews. Books from independent presses rely on reader-to-reader communications.

For more information or to order any of our books, visit:
http://www.fomitepress.com/our-books.html

More poetry from Fomite...
Anna Blackmer — *Hexagrams*
L. Brown — *Loopholes*
Sue D. Burton — *Little Steel*
Christine Butterworth-McDermott — *Evelyn As*
Christine Butterworth-McDermott — *The Spellbook of Fruit and Flowers*
David Cavanagh— *Cycling in Plato's Cave*
Raj Chakrapani — *The Repetition of Exceptional Weeks*
James Connolly — *Picking Up the Bodies*
Benjamin Dangl — *A World Where Many Worlds Fit*
Greg Delanty — *Behold the Garden*
Greg Delanty — *Loosestrife*
Mason Drukman — *Drawing on Life*
J. C. Ellefson — *Foreign Tales of Exemplum and Woe*
Anna Faktorovich — *Improvisational Arguments*
Barry Goldensohn — *Snake in the Spine, Wolf in the Heart*
Barry Goldensohn — *The Hundred Yard Dash Man*
Barry Goldensohn — *The Listener Aspires to the Condition of Music*
Barry Goldensohn — *Visitors Entrance*
R. L. Green — *When You Remember Deir Yassin*
KJ Hannah Greenberg — *Beast There—Don't That*
John Hawkins — *Mirror to Mirror*

Fomite

Fomite

Manufactured by Amazon.ca
Acheson, AB